Clever Kid Guide to Common Myths

S.E. Harrison

Published by Bow River Books, an imprint of Deep Stance Media
Calgary, Alberta, Canada
www.bowriverbooks.com

Print Book ISBN 978-1-998568-06-2
E-Book ISBN 978-1-998568-07-9
Version 1.0

Book written and designed by S.E. Harrison
Illustrations generated by DALL-E, an AI program developed by OpenAI

**Dedicated to those who
never stop seeking the
truth.**

Introduction

Welcome to the *Clever Kid Guide to Common Myths*! Have you ever heard something so many times that you just assumed it must be true? Well, you're not alone! Many of us believe things that sound believable, simply because they've been passed down from one person to another for generations. These stories, also known as myths, often start with a tiny misunderstanding or mix-up, and over time, they grow into "facts" that lots of people believe—even though they aren't true at all!

Common myths can come from a variety of places—old tales, misunderstandings of science, or even just guessing about how the world works. Sometimes, they spread because they're simple to explain or because they give people a sense of comfort, even if they're not accurate. You might hear them from friends, in movies, or even in school! But the thing about myths is, no matter how popular they are, they're still myths.

That's what makes learning about common myths so fun and educational. Once you discover the truth behind these widespread ideas, you'll start to see the world in a new way—one where not everything you hear is what it seems. It's like solving a mystery or uncovering a hidden secret! Plus, knowing the facts can help you avoid mistakes and impress your friends with your clever knowledge.

Most importantly, it's a reminder that just because a lot of people believe something doesn't mean it's true. We should always take the time to look into the truth behind what we're told, even if it's something we've heard our whole lives. Asking questions, doing research, and learning from reliable sources can help us find the real answers. So, get ready to bust some myths, laugh along with the illustrations, and become an expert myth-buster!

Are you ready to find out what's fact and what's fiction? Let's get started!

WHERE IS IT?

Myth:

The Great Wall of China is visible
from space.

Fact:

No human-made structure is visible from
space with the naked eye, including the
Great Wall.

Myth:

All dinosaurs were gigantic.

Fact:

Some dinosaurs were as small as chickens, while others were large.

BATS

Myth:

Bats are blind.

Fact:

Bats can see, and some even have
excellent vision.

Myth:

You lose most of your body heat
through your head.

Fact:

You lose heat through any exposed part
of your body, not just your head.

DON'T
FORGET!

Myth:

Goldfish only have a three-second memory.

Fact:

Goldfish can remember things for months!

Myth:

Lightning never strikes the same place twice.

Fact:

Lightning can strike the same place more than once, especially tall structures.

ONLY
10%

Myth:

We only use 10 percent of our brains.

Fact:

We use almost all parts of our brain, just not all at once.

Myth:

Eating carrots will give you night
vision.

Fact:

While carrots are good for your eyes,
they won't give you superhero-like vision.

Myth:

Chameleons change color to match their surroundings.

Fact:

Chameleons change color to communicate or to regulate their body temperature.

Myth:

Cracking your knuckles causes
arthritis.

Fact:

Cracking knuckles doesn't cause
arthritis, but it might annoy people!

Myth:

The moon has a "dark side."

Fact:

The moon rotates, so all sides get sunlight at different times.

Myth:

Gum stays in your stomach for seven
years if swallowed.

Fact:

Gum doesn't stay in your stomach—it
passes through your system like
other food.

Myth:

A dog's mouth is cleaner than a
human's.

Fact:

Both humans and dogs have bacteria in
their mouths, just different kinds.

Myth:

Bulls get angry when they see the
color red.

Fact:

Bulls are colorblind to red and react to
the movement, not the color.

Myth:

Humans evolved from monkeys.

Fact:

Humans and monkeys share a common ancestor but evolved separately.

Myth:

Sharks can smell a drop of blood from miles away.

Fact:

Sharks have a great sense of smell, but not that great.

EVEREST

Myth:

Mount Everest is the tallest mountain
in the world.

Fact:

Everest is the tallest above sea level, but
Mauna Kea in Hawaii is taller from base
to summit.

Myth:

Ostriches bury their heads in the
sand.

Fact:

Ostriches don't bury their heads—they
lie flat to avoid predators.

Myth:

Humans have only five senses.

Fact:

Humans actually have more than five senses, including balance and temperature.

Myth:

Touching a toad gives you warts.

Fact:

Warts are caused by a virus, not toads.

POP

Myth:

Eating pop rocks with soda will make your stomach explode.

Fact:

This is just a myth—your stomach can handle it.

Myth:

Houseflies live for only 24 hours.

Fact:

Houseflies live about 20 to 30 days.

Myth:

Hair grows back thicker after shaving.

Fact:

Shaving doesn't change the thickness, color, or growth rate of hair.

Myth:

Sugar makes kids hyper.

Fact:

There's no scientific proof that sugar causes hyperactivity in kids.*

*This answer sponsored by the sugar industry (just kidding!).

Myth:

You shouldn't swim right after eating.

Fact:

It's perfectly safe to swim after eating, though you might feel more comfortable waiting a bit.

Myth:

Birds will abandon their babies if
humans touch them.

Fact:

Most birds won't abandon their young
just because of human touch.

Myth:

Hair and fingernails keep growing after
death.

Fact:

They don't grow—the skin shrinks,
making it look like they're longer.

Myth:

The sun is yellow.

Fact:

The sun is actually white, but it appears
yellow due to Earth's atmosphere.

NORTH
SOUTH

Myth:

Water drains in opposite directions in the Northern and Southern Hemispheres.

Fact:

The direction water drains depends on the shape of the basin, not the hemisphere.

Myth:

You can catch a cold by going outside with wet hair.

Fact:

Colds are caused by viruses, not cold temperatures or wet hair.

Myth:

Lemmings commit mass suicide by jumping off cliffs.

Fact:

Lemmings don't intentionally jump off cliffs; it's a myth popularized by a documentary.

Myth:

Black cats are bad luck.

Fact:

Black cats are just like any other cat—no more or less lucky!

Myth:

Earth is perfectly round.

Fact:

Earth is an oblate spheroid, slightly flattened at the poles and bulging at the equator.

Myth:

Viking helmets had horns.

Fact:

Vikings didn't wear helmets with horns; this idea comes from costumes in the 19th Century.

Myth:

Space is completely silent.

Fact:

While sound doesn't travel through space like on Earth, radio waves and other signals can be "heard" by specialized equipment.

Myth:

Cats always land on their feet.

Fact:

Cats have a great righting reflect, but
they don't always land safely.

Myth:

If you swallow a watermelon seed, a watermelon will grow in your stomach.

Fact:

Watermelon seeds can't grow inside your stomach—it's too acidic!

Myth:

Brown eggs are healthier than white eggs.

Fact:

Brown and white eggs have the same nutritional value—the color just depends on the breed of chicken.

Myth:

You swallow spiders while sleeping.

Fact:

There's no evidence that people swallow spiders in their sleep—spiders avoid humans!

Myth:

Turtles can leave their shells.

Fact:

A turtle's shell is part of its body, so they can't leave it.

Myth:

Owls can spin their head in a full circle.

Fact:

Owls can rotate their heads about 270 degrees, but not a full 360.

Myth:

Chocolate causes acne.

Fact:

There's no direct link between eating
chocolate and acne.

Myth:

Eating before bed will give you
nightmares.

Fact:

While large meals might make you
uncomfortable, there's no proof they
cause you nightmares.

Myth:

Daddy longlegs are the most poisonous spiders, but their fangs are too short to bite.

Fact:

Daddy longlegs aren't spiders, and they're not venomous.

Myth:

You should drink eight glasses of
water a day.

Fact:

Hydration needs vary, and you get water
from food and other drinks, not just
water.

Myth:

Elephants are afraid of mice.

Fact:

There's no real evidence that elephants
are scared of mice.

SWEET
SOUR
SALTY
SALTY

Myth:

You have only one "taste zone" on your tongue for each taste (sweet, sour, etc.)

Fact:

All parts of your tongue can detect all tastes.

Myth:

Humans and dinosaurs lived at the
same time.

Fact:

Dinosaurs went extinct millions of years
before humans appeared.

Myth:

Chocolate is toxic to all animals.

Fact:

Chocolate is dangerous for dogs, but many other animals can eat it safely.

Myth:

People use different sides of their
brain for different tasks (left-brain vs.
right-brain).

Fact:

Both sides of the brain work together for
most tasks.

Myth:

Lightning always comes from the sky.

Fact:

Lightning can also go from the ground to the sky, known as ground-to-cloud lightning.

Myth:

Piranhas are vicious man-eaters.

Fact:

Piranhas are mostly scavengers and rarely attack humans.

Myth:

Drinking coffee stunts your growth.

Fact:

Coffee doesn't affect height, though it may affect sleep.

Myth:

Humans have only 206 bones.

Fact:

Babies have more bones and, as they grow, some bones fuse together.

Myth:

A coin placed on a train track can derail a train.

Fact:

A coin is far too small and light to derail a train.

Myth:

Goldfish turn white in the dark.

Fact:

Goldfish can change color due to
genetics and environment, but darkness
alone doesn't make them turn white.

Myth:

Plants grow better with music.

Fact:

There's no scientific proof that plants grow better when exposed to music.

Myth:

People in ancient times thought the
Earth was flat.

Fact:

Most educated people in ancient history
knew the Earth was round.

Myth:

Ducks' quacks don't echo.

Fact:

Ducks' quacks do echo, just like any other sound, but it can be harder to hear in some environments.

Myth:

If you touch a butterfly's wings, it
can't fly anymore.

Fact:

Butterflies can still fly if their wings are
touched, although it may harm them.

Myth:

Eating an apple a day keeps the doctor
away.

Fact:

While apples are healthy, they won't
replace a doctor's care.

Myth:

Wolves howl at the moon.

Fact:

Wolves howl to communicate with their pack, not because of the moon.

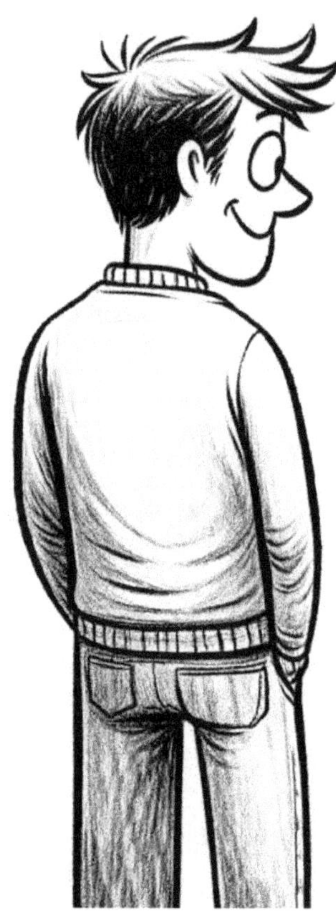

Myth:

A dog's wagging tail always means it's happy.

Fact:

Dogs wag their tails for various reasons, including excitement, nervousness, or even aggression.

Myth:

Licking a toad will cause
hallucinations.

Fact:

Most toads won't cause hallucinations;
only specific species have toxins that can.

Myth:

Bees can only sting once.

Fact:

Honeybees can only sting once, but other bees, like bumblebees, can sting multiple times.

Myth:

Birds explode if they eat rice.

Fact:

Birds can digest rice just fine; it doesn't
make them explode.

Myth:

Peanuts are a type of nut.

Fact:

Peanuts are actually legumes, not nuts.

Myth:

The moon is made of cheese.

Fact:

The moon is made of rock, not cheese.

Myth:

Napoleon was extremely short.

Fact:

Napoleon was about average height for his time period.

Myth:

Touching an electric eel will
electrocute you.

Fact:

While electric eels can deliver shocks,
they won't electrocute a person with a
single touch.

Z
Z
Z
Z
Z
Z
Z
Z

Myth:

Waking a sleepwalker can harm them.

Fact:

It's not dangerous to wake a sleepwalker,
but it can confuse them.

Myth:

Glass is a slow-moving liquid.

Fact:

Glass is actually a solid; its molecular structure doesn't flow over time.

Myth:

If you shave your cat, it will never grow fur again.

Fact:

A cat's fur will grow back after being shaved.

Myth:

An eagle can pick up a small child.

Fact:

Eagles are strong but not strong enough
to carry off a child.

Myth:

Touching poison ivy immediately gives
you a rash.

Fact:

You won't get a rash immediately; the oil
needs time to soak into your skin.

Myth:

You should pee on a jellyfish sting to stop the pain.

Fact:

Peeing on a jellyfish sting can actually make it worse. Vinegar is a better treatment.

Myth:

A goldfish will grow to fit the size of its bowl.

Fact:

A goldfish's size depends on its environment and genetics, not just the size of its bowl.

Myth:

Dolphins are always friendly to humans.

Fact:

Dolphins are intelligent but can be aggressive or territorial in some situations.

Myth:

Watermelons are 100 percent water.

Fact:

Watermelons are about 92 percent water, not completely made of water.

Myth:

Cows can predict the weather by lying down.

Fact:

Cows lie down for various reasons, but not to predict weather.

CROAK
CROAK
CROAK
CROAK

Myth:

A frog's croak can be heard miles away.

Fact:

Frogs can be loud, but their croaks don't travel that far.

Myth:

Bananas grow on trees.

Fact:

Bananas grow on large plants that are technically herbs, not trees.

Myth:

Wearing a hat causes hair loss.

Fact:

Hats don't cause hair loss, but tight ones might damage hair over time.

Myth:

Every snowflake is unique.

Fact:

While most snowflakes are unique, some snowflakes can be identical.

Myth:

Camels store water in their humps.

Fact:

Camels store fat in their humps, not water. The fat provides energy when food is scarce.

Myth:

Polar bears cover their noses with their paws while hunting.

Fact:

Polar bears don't hide their noses while hunting; they rely on stealth and patience.

Myth:

Chopping onions makes your eyes
water because of the smell.

Fact:

Your eyes water because onions release
sulfuric compounds, not because of the
smell.

Myth:

All deserts are hot.

Fact:

Some deserts, like the Antarctic Desert, are cold.

Myth:

A frog will stay in boiling water if
heated slowly.

Fact:

A frog will try to escape from hot water
as soon as it gets uncomfortable.

Myth:

If you drop food on the floor and pick
it up within five seconds, it's still safe
to eat.

Fact:

Bacteria can transfer to food immediately
upon contact with a dirty surface.

Myth:

Earthworms become two worms if cut
in half.

Fact:

Only one part of the worm may survive,
and it won't regenerate into two worms.

SPRING EQUINOX

Myth:

You can balance an egg on its end only during the spring equinox.

Fact:

You can balance an egg on its end any day of the year with patience and practice.

Z
Z
Z
Z

Myth:

Giraffes never sleep.

Fact:

Giraffes do sleep, though they sleep for
very short periods and usually
standing up.

Myth:

Eating celery burns more calories than the celery itself has.

Fact:

While celery is low in calories, it doesn't cause a calorie deficit just by eating it.

Myth:

Dogs are completely colorblind and see only in black and white.

Fact:

Dogs can see some colors, though their color vision is less vibrant than humans'.

Myth:

You can see the Eiffel Tower from anywhere in Paris.

Fact:

The Eiffel Tower is tall, but it's not visible from everywhere in the city.

Myth:

Lightning can't strike a car because of the rubber tires.

Fact:

Cars can be struck by lightning; the metal frame provides protection, not the rubber tires.

SUGAR

Myth:

Sugar causes cavities directly.

Fact:

Cavities are caused by bacteria in the mouth that break down sugars and produce acid, not sugar itself.

Myth:

Alcohol warms you up.

Fact:

Alcohol may make you feel warm, but it actually lowers your core body temperature.

Myth:

Bald men are more intelligent.

Fact:

Intelligence is not related to hair or baldness (but is related to how many *Clever Kid* books you read).

Please scan this QR code to leave a
review on Amazon:

Also from
Bow River Books

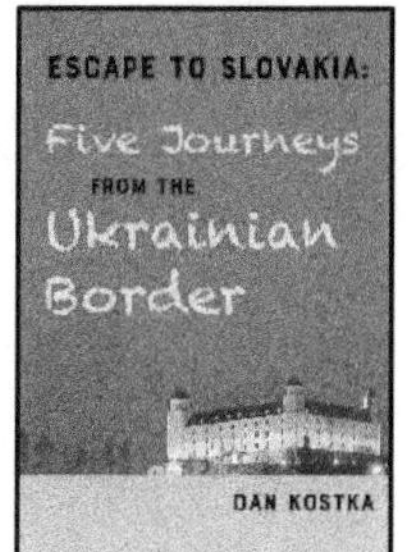

www.bowriverbooks.com